The Age of Dinosaurs

Meet Edmontosaurus

Written by Sheryn Knight

Illustrations by Leonello Calvetti and Luca Massini

Cavendish Square

New York

Published in 2014 by Cavendish Square Publishing, LLC
303 Park Avenue South, Suite 1247, New York, NY 10010

Copyright © 2014 by Cavendish Square Publishing, LLC

First Edition

This publication represents the opinions and views of the author based on his or her personal experience, knowledge, and research. The information in this book serves as a general guide only. The author and publisher have used their best efforts in preparing this book and disclaim liability rising directly or indirectly from the use and application of this book.

CPSIA Compliance Information: Batch #WW14CSQ

All websites were available and accurate when this book was sent to press.

Library of Congress Cataloging-in-Publication Data

Knight, Sheryn.
Meet edmontosaurus / by Sheryn Knight.
p. cm. — (The age of dinosaurs)
Includes index.
ISBN 978-1-62712-619-9 (hardcover) ISBN 978-1-62712-620-5 (paperback) ISBN 978-1-62712-621-2 (ebook)
1. Edmontosaurus — Juvenile literature. I. Knight, Sheryn. II. Title.
QE862.S3 D35 2014
567.913—dc23

Editorial Director: Dean Miller
Art Director: Jeffrey Talbot
Designer: Joseph Macri
Photo Researcher: Julie Alissi, J8 Media
Production Manager: Jennifer Ryder-Talbot
Production Editor: Andrew Coddington

Illustrations by Leonella Calvetti and Luca Massini.

The photographs in this book are used by permission and through the courtesy of: Image Source/Image Source/Getty Images, 8; Danita Delimont/Gallo Images/Getty Images, 8; Steve Lewis Stock/Photodisc/Getty Images, 8; David Henderson/OJO Images/Getty Images, 8; © AP Images, 20; Claire H./Edmontosaurus mummy/Edmontosaurs annectens/Creative Commons Attribution-Share Alike 2.0 Generic license, 21.

Printed in the United States of America

CONTENTS

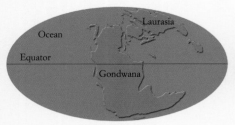

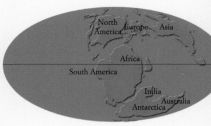

Late Triassic
227 – 206 million years ago.

Early Jurassic
206 – 176 million years ago.

Middle Jurassic
176 – 159 million years ago.

A CHANGING WORLD

Earth's long history began 4.6 billion years ago. Dinosaurs were among the most fascinating animals from the earth's long past.

The word "dinosaur" originates from the Greek words *deinos* and *sauros* and which together mean "fearfully great lizards."

To understand dinosaurs we need to understand geological time, the life time of our planet. Earth history is divided into eras, periods, epochs and ages. The dinosaur era, called the Mesozoic Era, is divided in three periods: Triassic, which lasted 42 million years; Jurassic, 61 million years; and Cretaceous, 79 million years. Dinosaurs ruled the world for over 160 million years.

| Late Jurassic | Early Cretaceous | Late Cretaceous |
| 159 – 144 million years ago. | 144 – 99 million years ago. | 99 – 65 million years ago. |

Man never met dinosaurs: they had disappeared nearly 65 million years before man's appearance on Earth.

The dinosaur world differed from our world. The climate was warmer, the continents were different, and grass did not even exist!

A DUCK BILL

Edmontosaurus was an Ornithischian dinosaur belonging to the group Hadrosauria, or hadrosaurians. Like Edmontosaurus, all hadrosaurians are called "duck-billed dinosaurs" because of the shape of their muzzles. Some, like Edmontosaurus itself, were flat-headed, but others had strange crests on the skull.

An adult Edmontosaurus could be more than 33 feet (10 m) long and 6 feet (1.8 m) high. Its weight was estimated at between 2.3 to 3.1 tons (2.1–2.8 t). Although it had no built-in defenses, its size and the fact that it lived in herds were a deterrent against most of its predators.

Edmontosaurus often moved on its hind limbs alone, thus it was bipedal or two-footed. However, it could also move on all fours, touching the ground with its forefeet as well as its hindfeet.

FINDING EDMONTOSAURUS

Edmontosaurus was among the last dinosaurs to populate Earth. It lived 70 to 65 million years ago at the end of the Cretaceous Period of the Mesozoic Era and it was 65 million years ago that large dinosaurs became extinct. The edmontosaurs populated North America, at that time divided in the middle by a sea crossing the whole continent, from the Gulf of Mexico to the north of Canada. Their remains are found from Colorado to Saskatchewan.

Alberta, Canada

Montana

South Dakota

Colorado

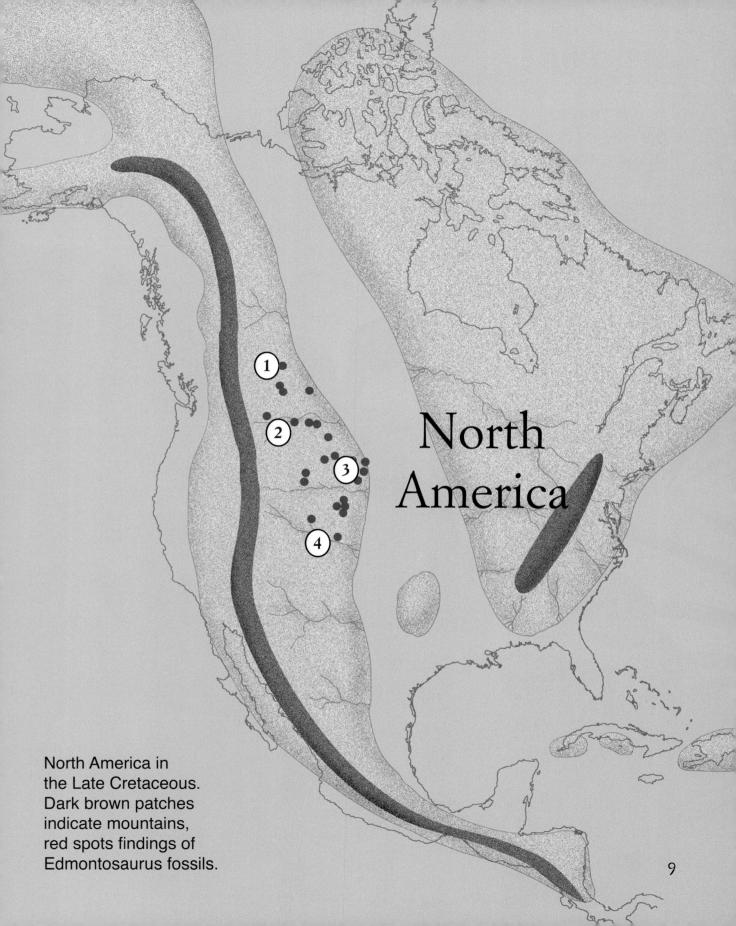

North America

North America in
the Late Cretaceous.
Dark brown patches
indicate mountains,
red spots findings of
Edmontosaurus fossils.

BIRTH

The hatchlings of Edmontosaurus came into the world from large eggs about 7.9 inches (20 cm) long. The young had short muzzles and large eyes. The eggs were laid at the bottom of a low nest that the mother had dug in the mud in open areas. These areas were far away from the forest and as protected as possible. Edmontosaurus nested in colonies, so the adults gathered could better defend eggs and hatchlings from the attack of predators.

LIFE LESSONS

Edmontosaurus was a gregarious, vegetarian dinosaur living in the wide coastal plains of North America. After an initial period spent in the nest where it received food from the parents, the young edmontosaur had to learn how to obtain food by itself. The young followed their parents in their first exploration of the surrounding world.

T-REX ATTACK

Edmontosaurus lived in a land populated mainly by vegetarian
dinosaurs, such as Thescelosaurus, Pachycephalosaurians,
and Ankylosaurians. Small bipedal predators such as Troodon
and Dromaeosaurus were not a problem for a herd of adult
edmontosaurs. They probably attacked only the young or the
eggs. The big danger for the duck-billed dinosaurs were the large
predators like the Tyrannosaurus or its close relative Albertosaurus.

LOOKING FOR FOOD

Edmontosaurus fed on needles and branches of conifer trees, seeds, and remains of other plants. The edmontosaur herds moved through the forest searching for food. To feed these large animals, an enormous amount of vegetation was necessary. However, attacks by meat-eating dinosaurs prevented the vegetarian dinosaurs from becoming so numerous that they would deplete the forest of all its vegetation.

INSIDE EDMONTOSAURUS

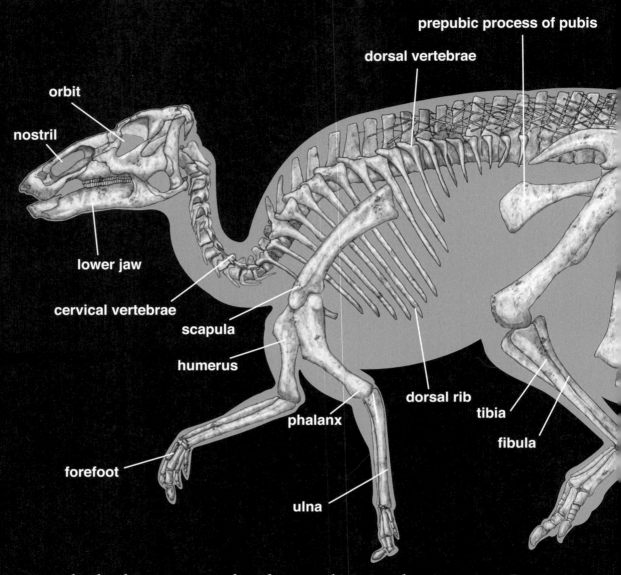

prepubic process of pubis

dorsal vertebrae

orbit

nostril

lower jaw

cervical vertebrae

scapula

humerus

phalanx

dorsal rib

tibia

fibula

forefoot

ulna

Edmontosaurus had robust jaws perfect for grinding tough vegetation. Its teeth were rather small, but numerous (some hundreds) and arranged in layers, so that when a row of teeth was worn, it was soon replaced by a new row.

The hind foot had three toes. The toes of the predator dinosaurs ended with a sharp claw, but those of the edmontosaur ended with flat, hoof-like nails.

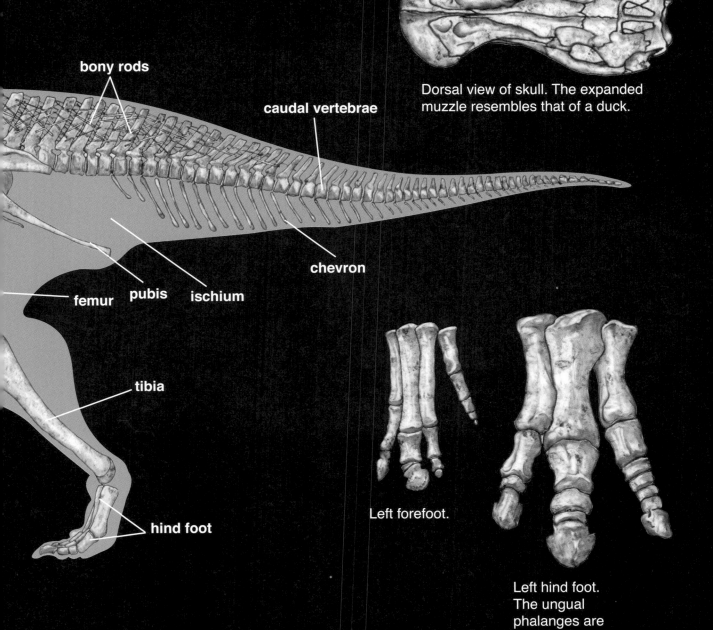

bony rods

caudal vertebrae

Dorsal view of skull. The expanded muzzle resembles that of a duck.

femur   **pubis**   **ischium**

chevron

tibia

hind foot

Left forefoot.

Left hind foot. The ungual phalanges are heart-shaped and flat.

FINDING EDMONTOSAURUS FOSSILS

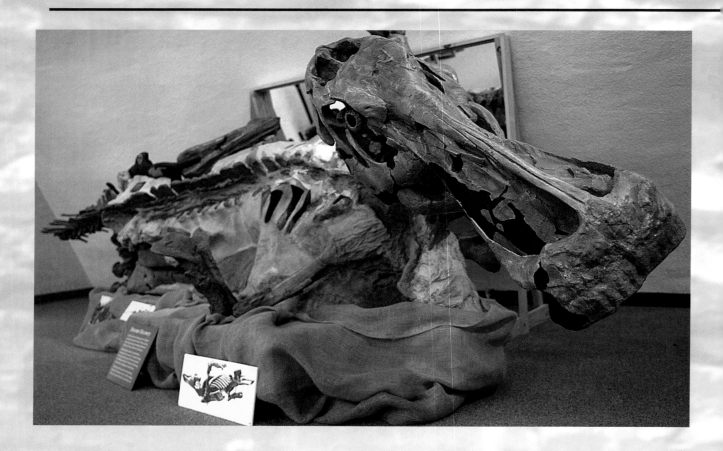

The first skeleton of Edmontosaurus was discovered in Montana in 1891 by the paleontologist and adventurous dinosaur-discoverer John Bell Hatcher. The name Edmontosaurus (meaning "lizard of Edmonton") was coined by the paleontologist Lawrence Lambe in 1917, in honor of the town of Edmonton in the Canadian Province of Alberta, where complete skeletons of this dinosaur have been unearthed.

George Sternberg made a sensational discovery in Wyoming in 1908 while he was digging for dinosaur bones. George found a skeleton still covered by its petrified skin. The fossil is now exhibited at the American Museum of Natural History in New York.

Edmontosaurus was very common along the coastal plains of North America as evidenced by the abundance of fossil remains in this area. It is one of the few dinosaurs known from many complete or nearly complete skeletons.

The "mummy" as exhibited today at the American Museum of Natural History in New York.

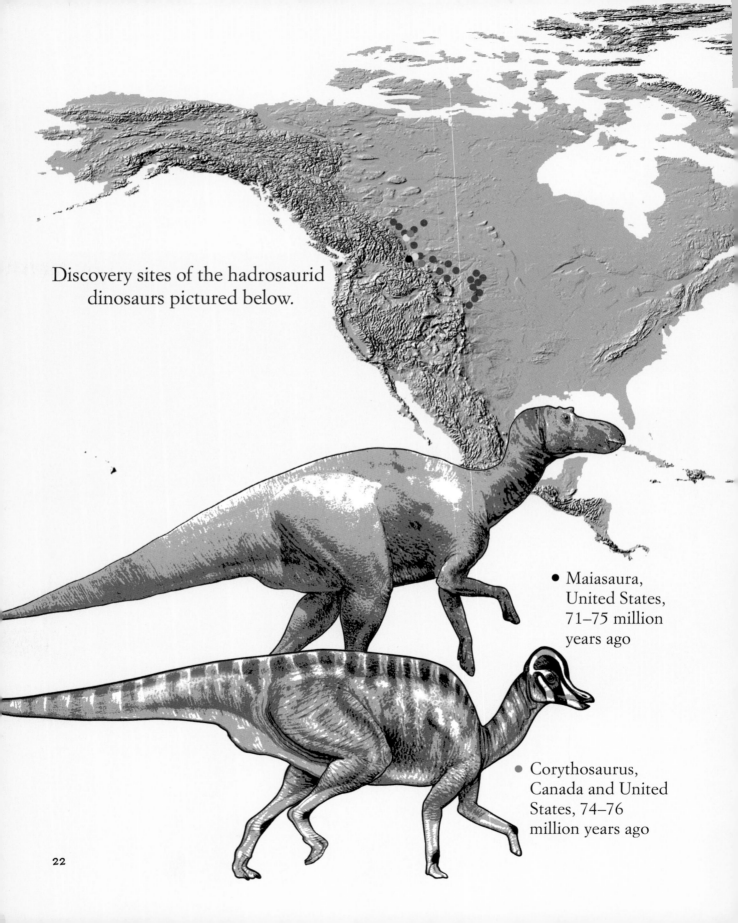

Discovery sites of the hadrosaurid dinosaurs pictured below.

● Maiasaura, United States, 71–75 million years ago

● Corythosaurus, Canada and United States, 74–76 million years ago

Lambeosaurus and Corythosaurus were crested hadrosaurids, while Maiasaura and Edmontosaurus were flat-headed.

THE HADROSAURIDS

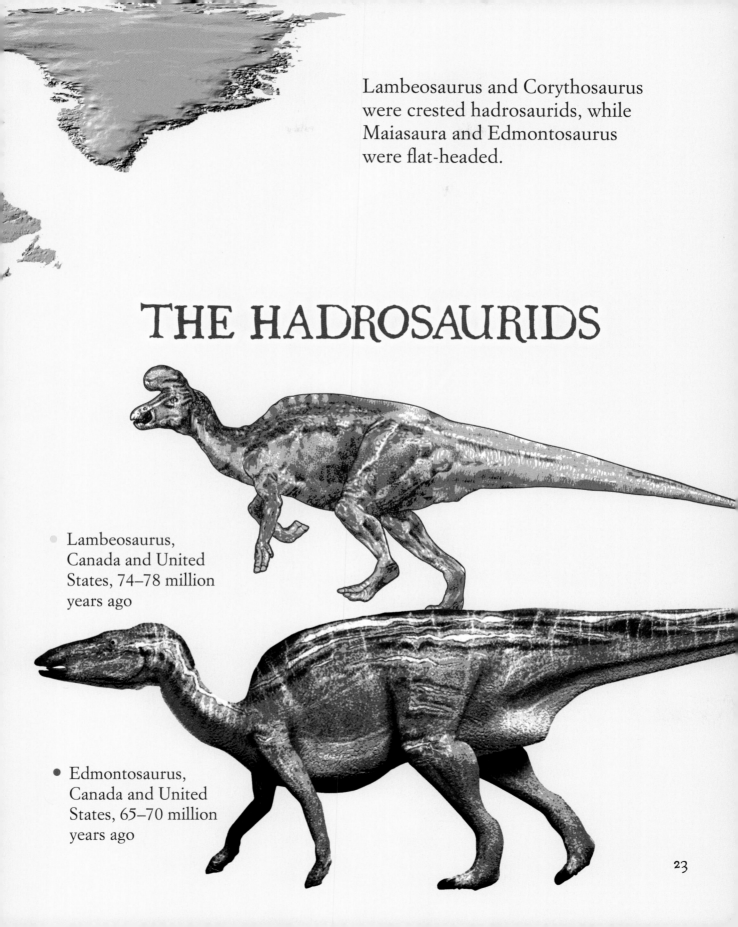

- Lambeosaurus, Canada and United States, 74–78 million years ago

- Edmontosaurus, Canada and United States, 65–70 million years ago

THE GREAT EXTINCTION

Sixty-five million years ago, when Edmontosaurus was one of the most common large animals on land, dinosaurs became extinct. Scientists think a large meteorite hitting the earth caused this extinction. A wide crater caused by a meteorite exactly 65 million years ago has been located along the coast of Mexico. The dust suspended in the air by the impact would have obscured the sunlight for a long time, causing a drastic drop in temperature and killing many plants.

The plant-eating dinosaurs would have starved or frozen to death. Meat-eating dinosaurs would have also died without their food supply. However, some scientists believe dinosaurs did not die out completely, and that present-day chickens and other birds are, in a way, the descendants of the large dinosaurs.

A DINOSAUR'S FAMILY TREE

The oldest dinosaur fossils are 220–225 million years old and have been found all over the world.

Dinosaurs are divided into two groups. Saurischians are similar to reptiles, with the pubic bone directed forward, while the Ornithischians are like birds, with the pubic bone directed backward.

Saurischians are subdivided in two main groups: Sauropodomorphs, to which quadrupeds and vegetarians belong; and Theropods, which include bipeds and predators.

Ornithischians are subdivided into three large groups: Thyreophorans which include the quadrupeds Stegosaurians and Ankylosaurians; Ornithopods; and Marginocephalians subdivided into the bipedal Pachycephalosaurians and the mainly quadrupedal Ceratopsians.

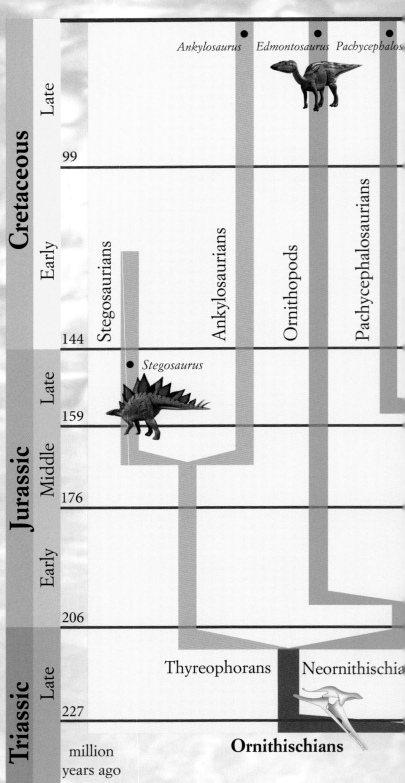

Ankylosaurus   *Edmontosaurus*   *Pachycephalos*

Cretaceous	Late	
	99	
	Early	
	144	
Jurassic	Late	
	159	
	Middle	
	176	
	Early	
	206	
Triassic	Late	
	227	

Stegosaurians   Ankylosaurians   Ornithopods   Pachycephalosaurians

Stegosaurus

Thyreophorans   Neornithischia

Ornithischians

million years ago

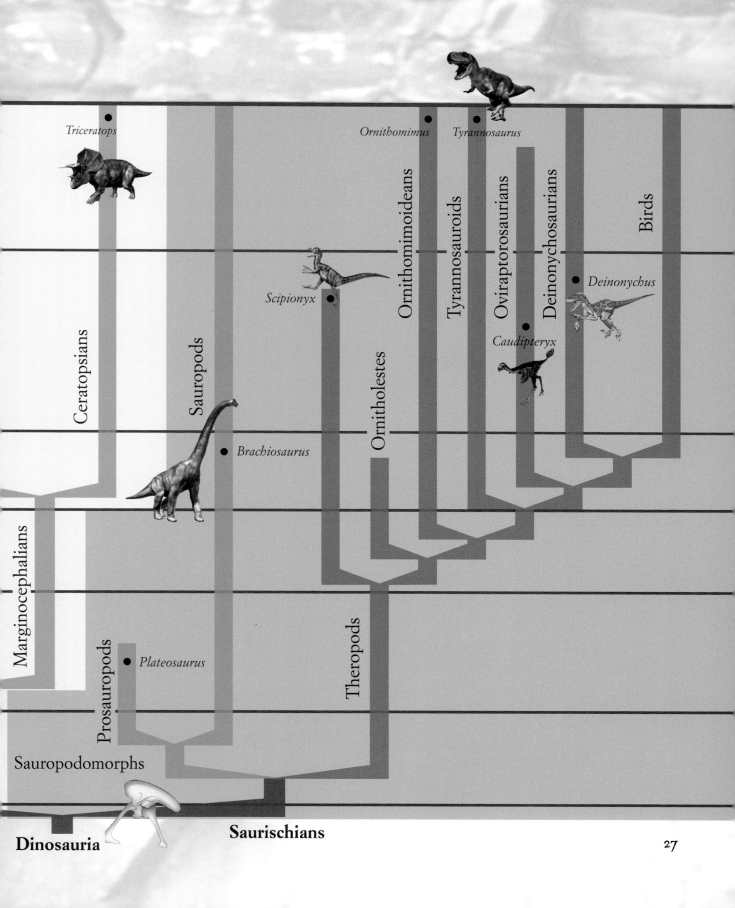

Triceratops

Ornithomimus

Tyrannosaurus

Ornithomimoideans

Tyrannosauroids

Oviraptorosaurians

Deinonychosaurians

Birds

Ceratopsians

Sauropods

Scipionyx

Deinonychus

Caudipteryx

Ornitholestes

Brachiosaurus

Marginocephalians

Theropods

Prosauropods

Plateosaurus

Sauropodomorphs

Dinosauria

Saurischians

A SHORT VOCABULARY OF DINOSAURS

Bipedal: pertaining to an animal moving on two feet alone, almost always those of the hind legs.

Bone: hard tissue made mainly of calcium phosphate; single element of the skeleton.

Carnivore: a meat-eating animal.

Caudal: pertaining to the tail.

Cenozoic Era (Caenozoic, Tertiary Era): the interval of geological time between 65 million years ago and present day.

Cervical: pertaining to the neck.

Claws: the fingers and toes of predator animals end with pointed and sharp nails, called claws. Those of plant-eaters end with blunt nails, called hooves.

Cretaceous Period: the interval of geological time between 144 and 65 million years ago.

Egg: a large cell enclosed in a porous shell produced by reptiles and birds to reproduce themselves.

Epoch: a memorable date or event.

Evolution: changes in the character states of organisms, species, and higher ranks through time.

Feathers: outgrowth of the skin of birds and some other dinosaurs, used in flight and in providing insulation and protection of the body. They evolved from reptilian scales.

Forage: to wander in search of food.

Fossil: evidence of the life in the past. Not only bones, but footprints and trails made by animals, as well as dung, eggs or plant resin, when fossilized, is a fossil.

Herbivore: a plant-eating animal.

Jurassic Period: the interval of geological time between 206 and 144 million years ago.

Mesozoic Era (Mesozoic, Secondary Era): the interval of geological time between 248 and 65 million years ago.

Pack: a group of predator animals acting together to capture the prey.

Paleontologist: scientists who study and reconstruct the prehistoric life.

Paleozoic Era (Paleozoic, Primary Era): the interval of geological time between 570 and 248 million years ago.

Predator: an animal that preys on other animals for food.

Raptor (raptorial): a bird of prey, such as an eagle, hawk, falcon, or owl.

Rectrix (plural rectrices): any of the larger feathers in a bird's tail that are important in helping its flight direction.

Scavenger: an animal that eats dead animals.

Skeleton: a structure of animal body made of several different bones. One primary function is to protect delicate organs such as the brain, lungs, and heart.

Skin: the external, thin layer of the animal body. Skin cannot fossilize, unless it is covered by scales, feathers or fur.

Skull: bones that protect the brain and the face.

Teeth: tough structures in the jaws used to hold, cut, and sometimes process food.

Terrestrial: living on land.

Triassic Period: the interval of geological time between 248 and 206 million years ago.

Vertebrae: the single bones of the backbone; they protect the spinal cord.

DINOSAUR WEBSITES

Dinosaur Train (pbskids.com/dinosaurtrain/): From the PBS show Dinosaur Train, you can have fun watching videos, printing out pages to color, play games, and learn lots of facts about so many dinosaurs!

The Natural History Museum (http://www.nhm.ac.uk/kids-only/dinosaurs/): Take a quiz to see how much you know about dinosaurs or a quiz to tell you what type of dinosaur you'd be! There's also a fun directory of dinosaurs, including some cool 3D views of your favorites.

Discovery Channel Dinosaur videos (http://dsc.discovery.com/video-topics/other/dinosaur-videos): Watch almost 100 videos about the life of dinosaurs!

Dinosaurs for Kids (www.kidsdinos.com): There's basic information about most dinosaur types, and you can play dinosaur games, vote for your favorite dinosaur, and learn about the study of dinosaurs, paleontology.

DinoData (www.dinodata.org): Get the latest news on dinosaur research and discoveries. This site is pretty advanced, so you may need a teacher's or parent's help to find what you're looking for.

MUSEUMS

Yale Peabody Museum of Natural History, 170 Whitney Avenue, P.O. Box 208118, New Haven, CT 06520-8118

American Museum Natural History, Central Park West at 79th Street, New York, NY 10024-5192

The Field Museum, 1400 So. Lake Shore Drive, Chicago, IL 60605-2496

Carnegie Museum of Natural History, 4400 Forbes Avenue, Pittsburgh, PA 15213-4080

National Museum of Natural History, the Smithsonian Institution, 10th Street and Constitution Avenue NW, Washington, DC 20560-0136

Museum of the Rockies, 600 W. Kagy Blvd., Bozeman, MT 59717

Denver Museum of Nature and Science, 2001 Colorado Boulevard, Denver, CO 80205

Dinosaur National Monument, Highway 40, Dinosaur, CO 81610

Sam Noble Museum of Natural History, 2401 Chautauqua, Norman, OK 73072-7029

Museum of Paleontology, University of California, 1101 Valley Life Sciences Bldg., Berkeley, CA 94720-4780

Royal Tyrrell Museum of Palaeontology, Highway 838, Drumheller, AB T0J 0Y0 Canada

INDEX

Page numbers in **boldface** are images.